46577030R00064

Made in the USA
Middletown, DE
30 May 2019